Making Life Right:

Reflections on Micah 6:8

Tim A. Dearborn

Table of Contents

Acknowledgements

1 The Great Requirement 1

2 Do Justice 12

3 Love Mercy 23

4 Walk Humbly with God 28

Eschatological Postscript: Great Consummation 37

Theological Foundations for Justice 40

Difference Between Social Service and Justice ... 42

About Micah Groups 43

Acknowledgements

Over 1,000 church leaders, from dozens of denominations and nearly every ethnic and socio-economic group in America, have joined a movement to discern how to live and lead at the convergence of worship, preaching, and justice. They are members of Micah Groups (www.micahgroups.org) in over 60 cities around the world. Men and women engage in courageous conversations about tough issues in an effort to discern how to do justice, love mercy, and walk humbly together with God. Twice a year facilitators of these groups gather at Fuller Theological Seminary in Pasadena, CA to reflect together on Micah 6:8. I'm grateful for the myriad ways they lead the church with creativity, boldness, and wisdom. The reflections in this booklet emerge from these times of worship, prayer, and interaction.

I'm also grateful for Mark Labberton, President of Fuller Theological Seminary. Mark launched Micah Groups with the vision for the church to surmount the barriers of denomination, ethnicity, and gender—and witness to God's reconciling, recreating love in the midst of all the complex issues in the world. Lloyd John Ogilvie has offered encouragement and inspiration through his lifetime of compassionate, courageous, wise preaching, and leadership. Jennifer Ackerman has brought creativity and insight in the shaping and implementation of the Micah Groups ministry. Finally, I am grateful for my wife, Kerry, who embodies steadfast love, wisdom, and humility. Throughout the ups and downs of life with me, she continually extends love and mercy.

1 The Great Requirement

I've spent hundreds of hours over the course of my life trying to discern God's will. Silent retreats, prayer, fasting, long walks in the woods and along city streets, pleading, "Show me your will, Lord. All I want is what you want."

Throughout these monologues, I wanted to hear God's voice, "Do this..." "Don't do this…." "Go here…" "Take this job…" "Don't take that one…" But so often, after hours of silence from my supposed dialogue partner, I'd finally only hear, "Draw near to me, and tell me what you want."

If I'd heard what God was thinking during these long agonizing journeys, it would probably be something like, "I've already shown you my will for most of your life. 98% of my will is crystal clear, fully known by you. Live into those aspects of my will that you already know, and you'll be easier to

To discern the will of God that we don't know, obey the will of God that we do know.

guide into the little bit you don't know." Or to put it more harshly, "Why should I show you more of my will when you're not obeying what I've already shown you." If I were God, I'd probably want to say, "You say, 'I only want your

1

will O God.' What you really want is for me to help you do your will. Sure, much of what you want is to serve me, in my kingdom. But your focus is on what you want/need to do for me, with me as your assistant to help you succeed. Your own ambitions, fears, desires for admiration and recognition shape your service, with me as the one who's expected to sanctify your efforts."

Does this sound too harsh? I don't think so. Frankly, not only can this be said of many of us individually, it can also be said of our churches. In our efforts to serve God, it's often our own church ambitions that are driving us. We seek God's blessing on our efforts—rather than focusing on how God is inviting us to participate in what God is already doing. Why else would we often be concerned with what church, organization, or leader gets the "credit" for good things that happen in the world? I believe we need continually to be reminded of the truth that our focus isn't on "our own" mission in the world. Rather, God has a mission in the world and we are invited to participate in it.[1]

Following the will of God that's already clear

To participate in God's mission we need to walk in God's ways. To discern those parts of God's will that we don't know, we may ask the Spirit to convict and empower us to live the will of God we already do know. Therefore, it's wise to ask "What are the dimensions of God's will (the 98%), that are already clearly evident?" I think much of God's is summarized in six great biblical affirmations.

---

[1] For more on our life as participants in God's mission, see Dearborn, *Beyond Duty: A Passion for Christ, a Heart for Mission* (Seattle: Dynamis Resources, 2nd edition, 2013).

1. The Great Commandment. *"Love the Lord your God with all your heart, and with all your soul, and with all your mind, and with all your strength, and your neighbor as yourself"* (Mk. 12:30; Mt. 22:37; Lk. 10:27). This command is so clear it needs little commentary. Do this, and we shall live. Lest we're uncertain what loving God and our neighbor looks like, Jesus continues to clarify God's will.

2. The New Great Commandment. *"I give you a new commandment, that you love one another. Just as I have loved you, you also should love one another. By this everyone will know that you are my disciples, if you have love for one another"* (Jn. 13:34-35). The world will believe we're Christ's disciples by our love for one another, and we are to love as Christ has loved us. And how does Jesus love us? The first is last, the greatest least, the other cheek is turned, and our life is given so that others' lives are made right. Rather than seeking to secure our own privilege and stature, if we love as Christ loves us, then we empty ourselves and live to serve others so that they might flourish (Phil. 2:1-10).

3. The Great Communion. This love leads to a new quality of relationships and community. *"May they all be one. As you, Father, are in me and I am in you, may they also be in us, so that the world may believe that you have sent me…I in them and you in me, that they may become completely one, so that the world may know that you have sent me"* (Jn. 17:21-22). Obeying God's great and new commandments leads to a quality of love for one another that will stun the world. This is the most compelling proof of the gospel the world will ever see.

3

4. The Great Commission. During his post-resurrection appearances Jesus gave what we've come to call the Great Commission. *"All authority in heaven and on earth has been given to me. Go therefore and make disciples of all nations, baptizing them in the name of the Father and of the Son and of the Holy Spirit, and teaching them to obey everything that I have commanded you"* (Matt. 28:18-20). God's will cannot be much clearer: teach everyone to obey Christ's commands. Teaching each other the will of God that we do know—the Great Commandment, New Commandment, Great Communion, and Great Commission. Our commission isn't simply to make believers of all nations, but disciples, followers, men and women who walk in the will and way of God.

Yet in case we're still unclear about how to do this, there's another "great" in the biblical description of God's will. We find this in the Old Testament Prophet Micah. Usually we jump right to Micah 6:8, *"God has told you, o mortal, what is good and what the Lord requires of you."*

Before exploring the implications of this verse, it's helpful to understand its context. Chapter 6 begins in the courtroom, goes to the temple, then the home, and ends up on the streets. The chapter opens with Micah declaring, *"The Lord has a controversy with his people"* (vs. 2).

"Ah, here it comes," many of us think. We go through life with the secret fear that God is upset with us. Somehow in the scales of God's will and holiness, we've not been enough, done enough, loved enough, and served enough. We live life shrouded in a sense of our own deficits and deficiencies, in spite of all the ways God demonstrates love for us. We have such a hard time believing we are lovable. Somehow, our attitude toward ourselves has more control in our lives than God's attitude toward us. So when we hear, *"The Lord has a controversy with his people,"* our guilt-laden perceptions are ready to be confirmed by what comes next.

> **Why do we let our opinion of ourselves be more emotionally determinative in our lives than God's opinion of us?**

While teaching a class on fasting, I suggested that there are other things we can give up besides food. People suggested various possibilities and agreed to try one the next week. When we reconvened, an older member of the class entered beaming with delight. "I've had the best week of my life. For my whole life I've continually sent myself 'you jerk' messages—criticizing myself for everything and anything. I fasted from that all week. When tempted, I simply reminded myself that God loves me. That was amazing. I've had the best week of my life."

It surprises us when we hear why God is upset. *"O my people, what have I done to you? In what have I wearied you?"* (vs. 3) God's controversy wasn't simply because of Israel's lack of obedience, lack of holiness, or lack of godliness. God grieves over Israel's lack of trust in God. This sounds very familiar to parents, who respond to a child's disobedience by wondering what they could have done differently so that the child believed that the parents' will was good. God's will is first and foremost for us to trust God, and not turn to anything else to prove our worth, justify our

5

existence, and ensure our security. The passage goes on (vs. 3-5), with God reciting some of God's mighty deeds to provide for and protect Israel—demonstrations over and over of God's trustworthy love.

In this courtroom of divine controversy, Israel interrupts, jumping to its own defense (vs. 6-7). How well I know that strategy. *"With what shall I come before the Lord?"* (vs. 6). What more can I do to please you God? In other words, maybe if I tried harder God wouldn't be upset with me. Israel launches into a frenzied list of things we could do to fix the problem of God being upset. First, Israel goes to the temple. Should we bring more sacrifices and offerings? Should we increase the passion of our worship? Invest in a new sound system for our church? Should I volunteer more time in ministry?

Hearing no response from God to their offer of more zealous worship life, Israel then goes to their family life. Should I sacrifice my children, *"the fruit of my body for the sin of my soul?"* (vs. 7) Tragically, that is often our response when we feel distant from God, or that our lives aren't bearing the fruit and gaining the recognition and admiration we desire. We work harder. We become more available to other people. We sacrifice our families and children to try to prove that we are trying hard and should be admired as dedicated Christians. I write this not as judgment of others, but as confession of my own sin. As church leaders we are especially prone to this.

The difficulty we have as pastors to gauge whether or not we are doing a "good job" can lead us to make sacrificial busy-ness the measure of our effectiveness. No one dare criticize us, because look at how busy we are, how hard we're trying, and how good are our intentions. Fear, ambition, and the desire for affirmation create volatile fuels that propel us into action. Lamentably, we settle for the 4 "b's" of pastoral excellence: bucks in the offering plate, bottoms seated in our pews, bravos of gratitude and appreciation, and as few boo's as possible. We long to hear expressions of appreciation and gratitude for our lives and ministry. Sometimes we are tempted to measure the authenticity of our devotion to God by the size of our congregations, the hours we give in committed service, the enthusiasm (and attendance) of our worship services, and our disciplines of Bible study and prayer.

5. The Great Requirement. God interrupts our frenzied effort to make ourselves acceptable to God, speaking through Micah: *"He has told you, O mortal, what is good; and what does the Lord require of you but to do justice, and to love mercy, and to walk humbly with the Lord your God?"* (Micah 6:8). This is God's Great Requirement for our lives. This is part of the "everything" we are to teach one another to obey, as Jesus commissioned in Matthew 28.

Guided by the 98%

Before examining what it means to do justice, love mercy, and walk humbly with God, it's worth lingering over the assertion that these "Greats" show us most of God's will. I spent much of my childhood enjoying sailing. I built boats, raced boats, and dreamed of boats. I carved model boats and strategized sailing around the world. But dreaming and thinking about sailing doesn't get your face wet. In fact, it doesn't get you anywhere. And simply sitting in a boat tied up to the dock doesn't either. Neither thinking about sailboats, nor sitting on one makes you a sailor. That only happens when you push out from the dock and get the wind in your sails. But even that's not enough.

Even with a strong wind you can be kept from moving forward. If the bow of your boat points straight into the on-coming wind, with your sail neither on the left or the right, you are simply flapping in the breeze and caught "dead center." "Dead in the water." Stay that way, and the wind may actually drive you backwards. As a result of poor planning, or indecision as to which way to turn, I've nearly been driven into other boats, and once almost onto rocks.

Don't follow the truth you know, and not only are you dead in the water and defeated, you can be driven backward and actually be dangerous. You have to turn one way or the other, point in a direction, and let your sails fill so you can get going. Only once you're moving forward can you turn the boat to head in a new direction. I think I've sometimes been unable to discern God's will because I've been stuck "dead center." I've been flapping in the breeze seeking guidance, paralyzed by indecision and uncertainty, dead in the water.

You can't turn a stationary ship.

Consider for a moment a major decision you or your family are trying to make right now: job, house, school for yourself or a child, where to volunteer your time, how to pay the bills, save for retirement, deal with health issues. Think of a major ministry or policy decision your church is trying to make: hiring a staff member, remodeling a building, changing the format or time of worship services, starting a new ministry, addressing issues of racism or economic injustice in your community, deciding about welcoming homeless people, refugees, or people in same sex relationships.

We want God's will. We want to rise above being controlled by our context, or being driven by fears and ambitions. Often in these situations, we search the Scriptures for applicable verses that might shed light. We ask God to speak to us words of guidance. We turn to wise counselors for input. All of this is good and right to do. But it is not enough.

At this point we need to hear, "obey the will of God that you know, and it'll be easier for God to move you in the direction God wants you to go."

- Am I asking the Spirit to empower me to love God with all my heart, soul, strength and mind; and love my neighbor as myself?
- Am I seeking to so abide in Christ that I love others with his love, the way he loves us?
- Am I inviting the Spirit to draw me close to the Father and Son, and to other people, so that our lives grow in oneness? In what ways is God leading me to grow in this?
- Is there anything in Jesus' commands that I'm avoiding?

Think once again of the issue for which you want guidance. Which action will enable you to participate more fully in God living out God's purposes in your life as expressed in these five greats?

The Great Commandment: love God and our neighbors,

The New Commandment: love one another the way Jesus loves us,

The New Great Communion: be one, even as the Father and Son are one,

The Great Commission: teach one another to obey everything Jesus taught us, and

The Great Requirement: do justice, love mercy, and walk humbly with God. (You may remember that I mentioned earlier that there are six *greats* revealed in Scripture to describe God's will. We'll explore the final one in the concluding section.)

Sometimes these don't necessarily shed clarity on the specific decision. They at least clarify the qualities and goals that God is calling us to pursue. These *greats* bring clear direction to the major qualities and the overall course that God wants to empower us to pursue in our lives. The wind of God's presence hits our sails and it becomes crystal clear which direction we need to go.

Follow the truth we know and God will guide us toward more of the truth we don't know.

Kerry and I were visiting friends from our church who were working as a doctor and nurse in the 100,000-person Khao I Dang refugee camp for Cambodians in Thailand. They did extraordinary work in their bamboo clinic, filling it medical care and kindness. Navy was one child for whom they were caring who was diagnosed with leukemia. This was far beyond anything they could treat. Without care he'd soon die. While our daughters were home drawing pictures of birds, and swings, and ponds—Navy drew machetes, machine guns, torture, and atrocities. The only way the US would allow him into the country was if a hospital would guarantee free medical treatment, and others would guarantee full financial support for his parents.

We didn't need to linger long in prayer to discern what to do. God's will seemed obvious to us. Kerry and I took his medical records with us. Soon upon our return home, Children's Hospital guaranteed treatment and our church small group rallied to provide the financial support so that Navy and his parents could live with us. There was nothing remarkable or exemplary in what we did. We were simply loving our neighbor as we would want to be loved. That simple decision charted a trajectory on the voyage of our lives that brought changes to our church, and to us personally. Our lives, very literally, have not been the same since an obvious decision made in a bamboo, thatched roof, and dirt floor refugee camp hospital.

In the next chapters we will linger over the three dimensions of God's good will set forth in the Great Requirement: to do justice, love mercy, and walk humbly with God. Through this, we'll understand more fully the 98% of God's will that is clear—and gain guidance for participating more fully in God making our lives and our world right.

2 Do Justice

"He has told you, O mortal, what is good; and what does the Lord require of you but to do justice, and to love mercy, and to walk humbly with the Lord your God?" (Micah 6:8).

Doing justice is not merely a set of activities that we add on to our lives as optional extras. Nor is justice the passionate preoccupation of, as some would label them, "progressive" or "liberal" Christians. Rather, doing justice, loving mercy, and walking humbly with God are the everyday lifestyle of all God's people. They describe what God regards as a "good life," a life lived right.

The Meaning of Justice

To do justice, we need to know what justice is. To understand justice, we need to see its relationship to mercy. Sometimes people are handicapped by the false notion that justice and mercy are opposites. Justice is viewed by some as the enforcement of the law, regardless of the cost. Mercy is viewed as granting clemency at the expense of justice. The image comes to mind of a courtroom where the judge deliberates between enforcing the demands of justice, or granting mercy. This common dichotomy threatens our engagement with biblical justice. Biblically, justice and mercy embrace. Thus the Psalmist pleads, *"Great is your mercy, O Lord; give me life according to your justice"* (Ps 119:156).

We are on a better path to understand biblical justice when we think in terms of the quality of our relationships and the content of our character, than by verdicts issued in a courtroom. In both Hebrew and Arabic, the words for justice and righteousness share common roots, describing the quality of character and conduct necessary for people to flourish in relation with God and one another.

Justice is rooted in the character and nature of God. The biblical faith affirms that God is love and God is just. God *loves* (Is. 61:8; Ps. 37:28) and *does* justice (Ps. 103:6; 140:12). The focus of God's justice is especially riveted on securing justice for victims of injustice—the poor, the marginalized, and the oppressed.

As God *is* just and loving, so we are to *do* justice and *live* in love (Amos 5:24; Deut. 16:20). The Bible reveals God as the One who pursues the marginalized to bring them home, who delivers the captives to make

Injustice is the abuse of power. Justice is power rightly ordered by love.

them free. Nothing in the Hebrew Bible more vividly discloses this than the Exodus account. Israel is continually called to *"Remember, you were once slaves in Egypt. Therefore, you must care for widows, orphans and strangers."* (Deut. 24:18-22) This is demonstrated over and over by Jesus as he heals people with leprosy, eats with social outcasts, and refuses to condemn those whom others judge. Jesus incarnates the fulfillment of the Psalmist's prophecy: *"Mercy and faithfulness will meet, justice and peace will kiss"* (Ps. 85:10).

Justice Makes Life Right

To do justice is to make life right. When we straighten a picture of the wall, we ad-just it. When we make the right hand margin straight on a page, we just-ify it. The same root. Justice is to adjust life to make it right, straight, and good.

To love our neighbor is to do justice. Those who are poor and victims of exploitation and oppression don't simply need charity. They need justice. Merely giving alms won't make life right and resolve the relational and structural (social, political, cultural, macro-economic, and even spiritual) contributors to their poverty and experience of injustice. The poor need justice, expressed in restored relationships and structural change, protection from exploitation, and access to opportunity.

One way of looking at this is to view justice as life being made right relationally and in society--outside us; and righteousness as life being made right personally— within us. Justice isn't first of all a legal term: *the measurement of our lives according to God's law and code of ethics.* Justice is a relational term: *people living in right relationship with God, one another, and the natural creation.* The goal of biblical justice is not the punishment of wrongdoers but the healing of persons and relationships.

> *Justice is for life to be made right around us. Righteousness is for life to be right within us.*

Justice and righteousness make life right. This requires the right ordering of power and relationships between people and in society (justice). However, that also requires the right ordering of power and relationships within people (righteousness). It makes sense that linguistically in the Bible, justice and righteousness share common roots. They are interdependent.

Without life being right within me (righteousness)—I may bring brokenness and pain to those around me. I risk inflicting my neediness, brokenness, and pain on those around me, or using them to fill up voids and needs within me—thus causing injustice.

Without life being right around me (justice)—I may experience damage to my own character, trust, and sense of worth. The misuse of power in poverty and oppression (injustice) does violence to the circumstances and the lives of both victims and perpetrators. It might do violence to their character and souls. People in chronic poverty often feel a flawed identity and diminished sense of personal worth.[2]

Doing justice isn't simply a commitment to occasional involvement in a good cause. It is our everyday lifestyle that begins within us (righteousness) and flows around us in our daily behavior as we participate in God's work of making life right.

To understand this more fully, it helps to recognize the progression in the biblical teaching about justice. Confusion occurs when we stop too soon, and do not see the full intent of God's will.

---

[2] Jayakumar Christian develops this idea in *God of the Empty Handed: Poverty, Power, and the Kingdom of God*, (Acorn Press, 2014).

The Beginning: Disproportionate Retaliation

The human norm in response to perceived injustice seems to have been (and some ways, remains) *disproportionate retaliation and revenge*. The story of Samson in Judges 14-17 illustrates this. Scorn me in my marriage and I'll destroy all your crops. Attack my family and me and I'll kill 1,000 of you. *"I will not stop until I have taken revenge on you"* (Judges 15:7). History is littered with the devastating debris of unending cycles of enmity and revenge. You hurt me and I'll extract as much from you as I possibly can. Attack our city and we'll destroy your country.

The Intermediate Step: Proportionate Retribution

On Mount Sinai, God introduced a radical improvement, replacing revenge with *proportionate retribution: "an eye for an eye, a tooth for a tooth"* (see Lev. 21:23-24; Deut. 19:19-21). The rule of law is better than brute power, domination by elites, or the whim of rulers. Consequences that are proportionate to the wrong done are far better than wholesale, unending hatred and slaughter. The enforcement of law so that perpetrators don't get away with injustice because of corrupt or ineffective law enforcement systems is a vast improvement over unrestrained oppression or revenge. Establishing the rule of law in societies is a major breakthrough to protect people's well-being, and contribute to rightly ordered power.[3] Without the rule of law, when revenge and the

---

[3] For a discussion of the integral connection between an effective criminal justice system and the alleviation of poverty and oppression, see Gary Haugen, founder of the International Justice Mission, *The Locust Effect: Why the End of Poverty Requires the End of Violence* (Oxford University Press, 2015).

abuse of power reign, society is perpetually unsafe. Restraining the vindictive impulse for revenge is essential and not easy. It's instructive that the Samson story occurs after God gave the law of proportionate retribution.

Justice as proportionate retribution is the norm in most civil law. Minimum sentencing regulations for courts set forth unwavering standards of what is determined to be proportionate punishment for offenses. In Islam, shari'ah expresses this view of justice, and many Christians also stop here in their approach to public justice. The presumed satisfaction of justice through capital punishment is the most lethal expression of this view of justice. That the strongest advocacy in America for the death penalty comes from evangelical Christians seems, to some, to be incongruous with the evangelical belief in God's extravagant love and restorative forgiveness.

The Goal: Disproportionate Love

Jesus Christ embodies and announces a third way, the radically different approach of *disproportionate love*. This forms the distinctive characteristic of a biblically rooted view of social justice and care for the poor. Jesus said, *"You have heard it said, "eye for eye, and tooth for tooth." But I say to you, do not resist an evildoer. But if anyone strikes you on the right cheek, turn the other also; and if anyone wants to sue you and take your coat, give your cloak as well...You have heard that it was said, "Love your neighbor and hate your enemy." But I say to you, love your enemies and pray for those who persecute you, so that you may be children of your Father in heaven...If you love those who love you, what reward do you have?"* (Matt. 5:38-46).

Making life right through disproportionate love has multiple dimensions. First, the victims of injustice need to

The strategy of Jesus appears naïve, weak, and foolish. Yet, the gospel proclaims this is the ultimate strength.

be made safe. They need to be protected from further harm, even if this means the restraint of the perpetrator. Disproportionate love doesn't mean that victims continue to submit to abuse and injustice. This neither makes life right for them, nor for the perpetrator. By continuing in injustice, perpetrators do damage (inflict injustice—unrighteousness) on their own souls, as well as on others.

Second, for their own sake, victims need to forgive their perpetrators. Otherwise, further damage will be done to them through bitterness and anger, doing injustice to their souls. Forgiveness precedes repentance, just as God's forgiveness of us precedes our confession. Even while people are enemies, as Jesus says, we still are empowered by the Spirit to love them. Love doesn't wait for people to apologize or become friends.

Third, love can even provoke and enhance the perpetrators' repentance and change of life. *"Do not repay evil with evil...If you enemies are hungry, feed them; if they are thirsty, give them something to drink; for by so doing this will heap burning coals on their heads"* (Rom. 12:17, 20). Justice is served and human life is made right—not merely by punishment of wrongdoers—but by merciful love, love for even our enemies. This is the very nature of the God of justice.

Fourth, this kind of love can lead perpetrators to the right ordering of their lives and of their relationships. Without repentance life won't be made right, but repentance isn't simply an apology. It is a change of life. For life to be right for themselves as well as their victims, the perpetrators need to work to repair the consequences of the damage they've done. To the extent possible, *Justice and love meet in Jesus' unrestrained love on the Cross and triumph in the resurrection.* without some kind of reparation, life won't be made right. This isn't simply proportionately punitive. Rather it's the opportunity for the perpetrators to express the same kind of disproportionate love as they have received.

For several years I was involved in World Vision's response to the devastating 2004 Asian tsunami. On one trip, I was meeting with the Islamic head of Shari'ah law in Aceh, Indonesia, to discuss issues pertaining to World Vision's involvement in this very conservative Muslim district. It was the same week as the 2006 massacre of five Amish girls in a school in Pennsylvania. In spite of their desperate efforts to recover from the tsunami that had struck their island the day after Christmas, killing in a few hours a quarter of a million people, local media in Banda Aceh was captivated by this news from America. First they reported it as further expression of decadence and violence in America. As the news from Pennsylvania developed, the Acehnese became spellbound by the response of the Amish.

Charles Roberts brutally killed five girls. The oldest girl he murdered, though still a child, with her hands and feet bound, asked to be shot first and to spare the other children. Yet half the mourners attending his funeral were related to the girls he killed. The Amish gave money and food to support Roberts' widow and children, since his death was also devastating for his family. Indonesians were riveted to the story of an Amish elder, saying to his community as he washed the body of his granddaughter, preparing her for burial, "The most important thing is that we must be careful not to have hatred in our hearts. Hatred is not our way."[4]

The director of Shari'ah was more interested in talking with us about the Amish than about World Vision. He said, "I'm speechless. I can't understand it. Do the Amish live this way because of their culture or their Christian faith?"

"Probably both," I replied. "Every morning Amish families read together Jesus' Beatitudes. Every Sunday they hear a sermon that includes some reference to Jesus' Sermon on the Mount and the call to love our enemies." He replied, "What would our world look like today, if around the world, we responded to injustice, violence, and enemies like the Amish?"

Executing a murderer, or punishing an offender, may seem at first to balance the scale, but it leaves someone, somewhere still suffering. The research is conflicted as to whether families of victims experience closure after the

[4] For more on this, see Donald Kraybill and Steven Nolt, *Amish Grace: How Forgiveness Transcended Tragedy* (Jossey-Bass, 2010).

perpetrator is executed.[5] Punishment, especially capital punishment, seldom gives the perpetrator the opportunity to make amends. Similarly, waging war against attackers or those who threaten us may bind up our damaged sense of honor, and may even deflect some further attacks, but violence rarely solves issues that provoked conflict in the first place. People restrained by violence or by threats are subdued captives, but not transformed people.

God calls us to protect and intervene on behalf of the weakest. As we do this, we are participating in the work of God. No wonder Jesus said peacemakers would be recognized as the children of God (Matt. 5:10).

Mercy lives between justice and humility. The way of unrestrained love makes sense only in light of the Cross. To be a Christian is to be convinced that in Jesus' death, God has borne the judgment for all injustice, all sin, and all the causes of suffering. In Jesus' resurrection, God has defeated all sin and evil and lifted all creation into new life. For many in the world, this is ridiculous, scandalous, and even blasphemous. Yet, Christians believe that Jesus willingly took upon himself the full weight of human and demonic evil, all disobedience to God, and all faithlessness. As we are crucified and raised with Christ (Romans 8, Gal.

---

[5] See for example, a report on a 2014 study done by researchers at the University of Texas at Austin, and University of Minnesota that indicates execution does little to heal families of victims (http://psychcentral.com/news/2014/01/26/study-finds-executions-do-little-to-heal-victims-families/64973.html). Debate.org has a running poll on the subject; the results are split 50/50 (http://www.debate.org/opinions/do-families-of-victims-feel-justice-with-the-death-penalty).

2:20), the Spirit empowers us to participate in this injustice-bearing character of God.

Pursuing justice for those who are treated unjustly is a decisive mark of following the will and way of God. Scripture does not merely measure faithfulness by our professions of orthodox doctrine or theology, by the zeal of our worship, or by the size of our religious buildings. Our faithfulness is most credibly expressed by how we make life right for those on the margins, for there power is most frequently abused.

In order to do justice God's way, we can't separate justice from mercy and humility. Justice by itself can make us seem tough and uncompromising. Mercy by itself can make us seem soft and sentimental, and blind us to the causes of injustice. Humility by itself can leave us trampled on and exploited by others. Making life right requires living all three dimensions of God's Great Requirement: doing justice, loving mercy, and walking humbly with God. Because justice is power rightly ordered by love, it's something we do, or more accurately, something in which we participate. Justice isn't an idea or a cause. It's a way of life as we with the God who loves justice.

3 Love Mercy

"He has told you, O mortal, what is good; and what does the Lord require of you but to do justice, and to love mercy, and to walk humbly with the Lord your God?" (Micah 6:8).

I'll never forget a conversation I had years ago with a pastor who grew up in a very rough neighborhood. When they left home in the morning to go to school, there was always the cloud of uncertainty hanging over their heads. Would they be caught up in random violence? Would the police stop them simply because of their ethnicity? Would they all make it home for dinner? Before leaving the door, their father gathered his children, prayed over them, and said the same thing each day: "Whatever happens today, never forget this: God is kind."

Remember, God is kind.

How often do we reflect on that as an attribute of God? Sovereign, powerful, all knowing, even loving—but kind?

In his book, *The Name of God is Mercy,* Pope Francis reminds us that God is *"rich in mercy"* (Eph. 2:4).[6] We walk with the God who is *"merciful, gracious, slow to anger, and abounding in steadfast love and faithfulness"* (Exodus 34:6). This verse uses the two great Hebrew words for mercy. The first word translated here as *"merciful,"* bears the same

---

[6] Pope Francis, *The Name of God is Mercy,* (Random House, 2016).

Hebrew root as the word "*womb*." Aspects of our current national and even international mood (whether in the church, in society, or in political debates) seem anything but merciful—harsh, anxious, divisive, name-calling, fear mongering—but not merciful.

Like a womb, mercy involves sacrifice, hospitality, discomfort, and even risk. Jesus stooped down and took the risk, so to speak, of bearing our wounded human flesh. He carried it into his own "womb of mercy" where it could be healed, redeemed, and recreated. His cries on the Cross were like labor pains, and in the resurrection, he gave birth to new humanity.[7]

Like a womb, mercy creates a safe place in which life can be nourished and made right.

The second word sometimes translated as "mercy" or "kindness" is translated in Exodus 34 as "steadfast love and faithfulness." This is the great Hebrew word, *hesed*, one of the most common words in the Hebrew Bible to describe God. God is steadfastly faithful to God's commitment to love creation. *Hesed* is God's resolutely faithful love. *Hesed* is the word translated in Micah 6:8 as mercy or kindness. What does God require of us—*"to do justice, love mercy (hesed), and walk humbly with God."*

God calls us to participate in God's unconditional, relentless, unwavering, steadfast determination to heal the

---

[7] For reflections on this, see the writing of the 15th Century British theologian and mystic, Julian of Norwich, *Revelations of Divine Love* (Penguin Books, 1999).

wounds of humanity in God's love. When we walk the way of justice, mercy, and humility, we courageously participate in God creating safe places in which people's lives can be made right by mercy.

Pope Francis calls for *A Year of Mercy*. "God forgives not with a decree but with a caress" (p. xii), for "Jesus goes beyond the law and forgives by caressing the wounds of our sins." Only the person "who has been touched and caressed by the tenderness of his mercy really knows the Lord. For this reason I have often said that the place where my encounter with the mercy of Jesus takes place is my sin. When you feel his merciful embrace…that's when life can change" (p. 34).

"To follow the way of the Lord, the Church is called on to pour its mercy over all those who recognize themselves as sinners, who assume responsibility for the evil they have committed, and who feel in need of forgiveness…The Church does not exist to condemn people but to bring about an encounter with the

Mercy creates communities where all life can be protected and nourished.

visceral love of God's mercy. I often say that in order for this to happen, it is necessary to go out: to go out from the church and its parishes, to go outside and look for people where they live, where they suffer, and where they hope" (p. 52).

The Spirit is at work to deepen our transformation in the womb of God's mercy so that we can lead the Church in this great "revolution of tenderness." Frequently in the New Testament mercy and new birth are connected. *"By*

God's great mercy he has given us a new birth into a living hope through the resurrection of Jesus Christ" (1 Pet. 1:3). *"When the goodness and loving-kindness of God our Savior appeared, he saved us, not because of any works of righteousness that we had done, but according to his mercy, through the water of rebirth and renewal by the Holy Spirit"* (Titus 3:4).

The call to love mercy, to love kindness, reminds us that we don't live in the courtroom of judgment, or only in the classroom of good moral advice. We live in the bridal chamber of God's tender mercy, where God draws us into the recreating embrace of God's love to give birth to new life.[8]

Dorothy was a World Vision staff member in Rwanda. During the genocide, she was in her house with her children when a mob came down the street. Somebody burst into her house, dragged her son outside, and killed him with a machete in her front yard. Every day, Dorothy prayed for her son's murderer, and for all the other victims and perpetrators of that horrible 100 daylong massacre of 100,000 people. Many, both victims and murderers, were followers of Christ, neighbors, friends, and associates of one another. For a few weeks, the rage of fear and partisanship was more powerful than the blood and Spirit of Christ.

---

[8] For a profound development of how mercy and justice bring those who feel marginalized and rejected into the ballroom of God's Kingdom, see Fr. Gregory Boyle, *Tattoos on the Heart: The Power of Boundless Compassion* (Free Press, 2011).

A decade after the genocide, there was a furtive knock on Dorothy's door. She opened it and who should be there, but the man who had killed her son. He said, "I've come here that justice would be done. I killed many people during those hundred days, but for 10 years I've not been able to get the face of your son out of my mind. So I'm here for you to take me to the police and let justice be done."

Dorothy opened her door wider and pulled the man inside her home. She said to him, "Young man, justice will be done. You took away my son. You shall now be to me as a son."

Christ draws us into the womb of God's love to renew, recreate, and restore us. Mercy creates a safe place where God's right-making justice can work. When that happens, we draw one another into the banquet hall of God's coming kingdom, where we can feast on the goodness of God. The kindness of God has appeared.

4 Walk Humbly with God

"He has told you, O mortal, what is good; and what does the Lord require of you but to do justice, and to love mercy, and to walk humbly with the Lord your God?" (Micah 6:8).

"Walk humbly with the Lord your God." Our English word for humility shares the same linguistic root as "soil" (*humus*). Justice, mercy, and humility meet when my hands and feet are soiled with the needs of the world, and with my own ordinary humanity. They meet when we, *"in humility, regard others as better than yourselves"* and *"Let the same mind be in you that was in Christ Jesus,"* who, *"being found in human form, he humbled himself and became obedient to the point of death—even death on a cross"* (Phil. 2:3-5, 8). Justice, mercy, and humility meet when we recognize that we stand on the same ground as others, level, equally in need of the mercy and kindness, the steadfast love of God.

In Galatians 5:22, humility isn't listed as a fruit of the Spirit. Rather than a fruit of the Spirit, humility is a fruit of facing reality. When we honestly see ourselves in our weakness, vulnerability, and dependency, we will be humble. Or, to be more honest, we will recognize and admit what's always been true about us—our humility. If humility is the fruit of facing reality, not being humble is the fruit of deception. It relies on avoiding or denying

Humility isn't a fruit of the Spirit. It's a fruit of facing reality.

reality. Admitting our humility requires removing the defenses we've erected to hide from ourselves and from others our weakness, ordinariness, and vulnerability. That's often done only through suffering and pain. It's seldom easy. For some of us, we struggle to hold on to our armor, even when it is God's love and the call to freedom that bid us to let go.

Humility often feels like a virtue when we see it in others, but like a weakness when we see it in ourselves. This is especially true in cultures that exalt pride, and commend confidence, fame, and even arrogance as signs of power. The ego resists dying, and usually only with great struggle, even at the hands of

The strongest barriers to owning our humility are dishonesty and pride.

unconditional love. As Fr. Richard Rohr says, "The ego hates losing, even to God."[9]

Gregory of Nyssa, a 4th century theologian in the Early Church, wrote, "Unlike every other aspect of God's nature, which goes far beyond the limits of our nature, humility is something that is natural to us... But don't think humility is something that can be achieved easily or without practice. Quite the opposite: humility requires more practice and effort than any other highly sought after character quality. Why? Because humility's opposite—the sin of pride—is deeply engrained in our being...I want to be clear about this issue: there is no evil that so wounds

---

[9] Richard Rohr, *Falling Upward: Spirituality for the Two Halves of Life* (John Wiley and Sons, 2011), 47.

our soul as pride."[10]

More recently, C.S. Lewis commented, "The utmost evil is Pride. Unchastity, anger, greed, drunkenness, and all that, are mere fleabites in comparison. It was through Pride that the devil became the devil."[11]

Humility is seen in how we walk

The intersection of justice, mercy, and humility is in our feet and hands (not just our words). The way to confront

"Pride is your greatest enemy, humility is your greatest friend."
John R.W. Stott

the arrogance of power and pride in ourselves, others, and systems and society is by walking humbly. Prophetic denouncements can be seen as arrogant. Chastising warnings against injustice can be seen as self-righteous.

Kerry and I saw what it means to live in the humble, joyful, confidence of Christ through a woman Kerry met in Beijing. We had the privilege of taking a group from our church to China shortly after that country was opened to tourists following the Cultural Revolution. We informed the tourist officials that we were a Christian group and wanted to learn as much about the church in China as possible. They obliged, and many extraordinary encounters followed.

Kerry had a conversation after church one Sunday with

---

[10] Gregory of Nyssa, *Sermons on the Beatitudes*, paraphrase by Michael Glerup, (InterVarsity Press, 2012), 27-28.
[11] C.S. Lewis, *Mere Christianity* (Simon and Shuster Edition, 1996), 109, 111.

one of the first woman physicians in China. During the Cultural Revolution, she'd been doubly disdained, first for being highly educated and second for being a Christian. For three years she was assigned the humiliating task of sweeping streets in a rural village, in spite of the obvious need for doctors. Her high quality work outraged her keepers. Not only did she sweep the streets thoroughly, she did it joyously.

She eagerly recounted to Kerry a conversation with her guards, when in exasperation they asked, "Why are you so happy? You, a mighty doctor, should feel utterly humiliated." She answered, "I can sweep streets for the glory of God and the good of my country, or I can take care of people's health. Either way, it is to God's glory. You choose how I might serve."

We walk receptively. The humble are open, responsive, and eager to be changed by the character and kindness of God. They live with vulnerable hearts. The humble know that they don't know everything. They are comfortable admitting their poverty, dependency, neediness, and weakness. It shouldn't be surprising therefore that Jesus said it's the poor in spirit who receive the Kingdom of God (Mt. 5:3), and that Paul rejoiced that our acknowledged weakness becomes the dwelling place for God's power (2 Cor. 3:5; 4:7; and 12:9). God *"said to me, 'My grace is sufficient for you, for power is made perfect in weakness.' So, I will boast all the more gladly of my weaknesses, so that the power of Christ may dwell in me."*

We walk silently. The root of the Hebrew word for

humility used in Micah 6:8 can also be used for the word "silently." This makes great sense. To be silent before God means many things: no self-justification or defense, no pride or pretense, no arrogance or presumption, no hiding behind excuses. Rather, we stand with open hands, in the freedom of honest dependency and trust.

The humble are free to walk receptively, responsively, courageously, and confidently. Those who are humble know that we are invited into God's presence because of God's *hesed*, God's steadfast love, and not because of the virtue or merit of our devotion or service. Furthermore, because it is in *God's* presence that we walk, to walk in humility is actually to walk strong. Hundreds of millions of people have found comfort in the oft-quoted verse, *"Though I walk through the valley of the shadow of death I fear no evil, for Thou art with me"* (Psalm 23). This capacity is nourished when we kneel before God in silent dependency, stripped of the self-righteousness and self-centeredness we vainly try to defend or assert. God assures us that we abide in God's presence and are empowered with God's strength.

Because of God's trustworthy love, we walk boldly in confident humility and gentle courage.

We walk courageously with God. Walking with God makes our acknowledged, essential humility safe. We don't walk alone. We may feel vulnerable, and exposed when we admit our weakness. But we're not on our own. We walk together with others and with God. We walk united with others in compassion, rather than divided in fear and enmity.

32

We walk with God because we, *"have been crucified with Christ; and it is no longer I who live, but it is Christ who lives in me. And the life I now live in the flesh I live by the faith of the Son of God, who loved me and gave himself for me"* (Gal. 2:19-20). Now through the Holy Spirit, we share in both his suffering and in his new life that reconciles all things to God—making life right.

The power of walking on level ground. In his book, *Just Mercy*, Bryan Stevenson tells a compelling story of the transforming power of humility.[12] Bryan has labored for decades as a civil rights attorney on behalf of victims of injustice in the US criminal law system. He has helped over 100 people to be set free from prison who were unjustly sentenced to death.

But this journey began, as he humbly confesses, knowing nothing about law, prisons, death row, or how to enable our so-called criminal justice system to be more just. The first time he met with someone on death row (and his first case ever) was as a young law student. There were other "firsts" to this encounter. He was the first attorney, and in fact, the first visitor this young man had received in two years since being sentenced to death. After the guards had slowly removed all the shackles from Henry's hands, waist, and feet, Bryan reached out to shake his hand. Bryan describes what happens next. "'I'm very sorry,' were the first words I blurted out. Despite all my preparations and rehearsed remarks, I couldn't stop myself from apologizing repeatedly. 'I'm really sorry...I'm just a law student, I'm

---

12 Bryan Stevenson, *Just Mercy: A Story of Justice and Redemption* (Random House, 2014), 9-11.

not a real lawyer...I don't know very much.'"

Then Bryan said the one thing he did know, that Henry had at least a year before he'd be executed. Henry was overcome with relief. "Thank you, man, I mean, really, thank you! This is great news." He hadn't wanted to let his wife and children come see him, fearing that the prison would set the date of their visit as the day he'd be executed. "I just don't want them here like that. Now I'm going to tell them they can come and visit."

Bryan relaxed and the two engaged in a three-hour conversation "about what's important in life and what's not." No longer separated by barriers as junior law clerk and condemned convict, they were two brothers talking about their lives and struggles. Finally, the guards angrily barged in. They roughly re-shackled Henry and started shoving him out the door. Bryan apologized, saying it was his fault that the meeting had gone so long, begging the guards not to be so rough on Henry. Henry said, "Don't worry about this, Bryan. Just come back." Then he stood so the guards couldn't push him through the door, threw his head back, and sang. Bryan comments, "It startled both me and the guards, who stopped pushing." Henry sang in the doorway, and all the way down the hall to his cell:

God's power is released when we humbly stand with others in shared brokenness.

> I'm pressing on, the upward way
> New heights I'm gaining, every day
> Still praying as I'm onward bound
> Lord, plant my feet on Higher Ground.

When we discover that we're brothers and sisters together—united in our common and ordinary humanness, with our relationships unobstructed by differences of class, ethnicity, or status—God's power is released. In the transforming womb of God's love, God restores us, and leads us to Higher Ground.

The dehumanizing rooms of prisons can become sanctuaries of communion. Whether we are shackled by chains or by our own feelings of unworthiness, shame and inadequacy, we can be lifted in worship of the God who inspires courageous hope. Our level ground becomes the pathway to Higher Ground.

We want to live life right. God has shown us what is good. We are reminded of Jesus' first sermon recorded in Luke 4:18-19: *"The Spirit of the Lord is on me because he has anointed me to bring good news to the poor. He has sent me to proclaim release to the captives and recovery of sight to the blind, to let the oppressed go free, to proclaim the year of the Lord's favor."*

> **"The opposite of poverty isn't wealth. It is justice."**
> **Bryan Stevenson**

We also hear some of his last words, as recorded in the Gospel of John 20:21-22: *"As the Father has sent me, so send I you...Receive the Holy Spirit."*

The Great Requirement doesn't end in the sanctuary but in the marketplace, the prisons, homeless camps, and workplaces of our world. As occurred with Bryan and Henry, the Spirit can transform these places into sanctuaries, altars, places of communion and worship. Micah reminds us in 6:9-12 that God's will extends from the sanctuary and home into the streets and marketplace.[13] We live out God's justice through our everyday, ordinary way of life as neighbors, employers, employees, customers, merchants, and manufacturers.

The Hebrew prophets continually stressed the sincerity of our worship on the Sabbath is measured by how we do business the rest of the week.[14] If we're doing God's will, our houses won't be filled with treasures gained in ways that oppress others. The payments we give for labor and for products will be honest and fair. Our affluence won't be at the expense of others' injury or harm. Our promises will be kept and our words will be true. As a result, our homes will be filled with *"righteousness, peace, and joy in the Holy Spirit."* (Rom. 14:17).

The Spirit is inviting us to live life well and participate in God making all dimensions of life right. This occurs as we enter into the womb of God's mercy, and allow God to make our lives and world right.

---

[13] For further development of this, see Dearborn, *Business as a Holy Calling?: A Workbook for Christians in Business and Their Pastors* (Seattle: Dynamis Resources, 2015).

[14] In addition to Micah 6, see Jeremiah 7: 1-11; Hosea 4: 4-7; Isaiah 1:17-21.

Eschatological Postscript:
The Great Consummation

There's a sixth *Great* in God's will. It's the one to which all the other Greats point. This is the one that emboldens our faithful submission to God's will and ways. It fuels our hope and feeds our courage.

The Great Consummation

Yet the biblical faith is founded and sustained by the conviction that justice is coming. Life will be made right. One day all injustice will end. *"God will dwell with mortals; they will be God's peoples, and God will be with them; God will wipe every tear from their eyes, Death will be no more; mourning and crying and pain will be no more...And the one who was seated on the throne said, 'See, I am making all things new.'"* (Revelations 21:3-5). One day all violence and abuse of power will be end. One day, lions and lambs, enemies and foes will dwell together in peace. One day we will gather around the throne of the Lamb who was slain for the injustices of the world, and who is now the Great Shepherd, leading us into the Banquet Hall of the Kingdom.

> **"Hopelessness is the enemy of justice."**
> **Bryan Stevenson**

Our capacity and courage to live the Great and the New Commandments, to share in the Great Communion, obey the Great Commission, and walk in the Great Requirement are fueled and fed by the Holy Spirit who reminds us of the Great Consummation. *"Hope does not disappoint us, because God's love has been poured into our hearts through the Holy Spirit"* (Rom 5:5).

In about 1850, Theodore Parker, a New England abolitionist and minister preached a sermon called "On Justice and the Conscience." In the midst of the struggle against slavery, he proclaimed, "God has made man with an instinctive love of justice...Look at the facts of the world. You see a continual

The arc of the universe bends toward justice.

and progressive triumph of the right. I do not pretend to understand the moral universe; the arc is a long one, my eye reaches but little ways; I cannot calculate the curve and complete the figure by the experience of sight; I can divine it by conscience. And from what I see I am sure it bends towards justice."

Parker goes on to say, "Injustice cannot stand. No armies, no 'Holy Alliance,' can hold it up. Human nature is against it, and so is the nature of God! 'Justice has feet of wool,' no man hears her step, 'but her hands are of iron,' and where she lays them down, only God can uplift and unclasp.

It is vain to trust in wrong."[15] Dr. Martin Luther King, Jr. paraphrased this over 100 years later in his 1958 speech, "Out of the Long Night." "The arc of the moral universe

---

[15] Theodore Parker, "Of Justice and the Conscience," *Ten Sermons of Religion by Theodore Parker*, (Boston: Crosby, Nichols and Company, 1853), 84-85, 87.

is long, but it bends toward justice."[16]

Sometimes that arc seems painfully too long. In so many situations, Parker's 1850 affirmation, and King's reiteration of it 50 years ago, still sound like affirmations of faith—confidence in what's yet unseen.

"May the God of hope fill you with all joy and peace in believing, so that you may abound in hope by the power of the Holy Spirit" (Rom. 15:13). Hundreds of thousands of churches and millions of Christians around the world are witnesses to this great hope, as the Spirit works through them to do justice, love mercy, and walk humbly with God—making life right. Together, we live with bold humility and gentle courage, for we know that the long arc of God's universe bends toward justice. We know this because the God of steadfast love is Lord.

---

[16] Martin Luther King, Jr., "Out of the Long Night," *The Gospel Messenger*, (Elgin: Brethren General Brotherhood Board, Feb 3, 1958), 14.

Theological Foundations for Justice

1. **God's nature:** God exists in a communion of Triune Love, establishing the way and pattern for just and harmonious sharing amongst humankind.

2. **Human nature:** All people exist in the image of God and therefore are to be treated with justice.

3. **God's will:** God loves all of God's creation and wills that all creation experience fullness of life in the shalom, justice, and reconciliation of God's kingdom.

4. **God's establishment of justice in Jesus Christ:** In the life, death and resurrection of Christ, God has acted decisively to defeat all that thwarts life from being right (just) and to establish God's kingdom of righteousness on earth.

5. **God's work through the Christian community:** God's call to Israel and now the Church is to be the community that demonstrates God's special commitment to those on the margins, the outsiders, the victims of injustice and oppression—for in so doing we demonstrate the nature of God and the quality of life for which we are created. Because justice involves human life in reconciled harmony, human participation as agents of justice is vital. Therefore, God chooses to work through people to establish justice.

6. **God's work through the Spirit:** God is not restricted to human agency. It is the work of the Spirit to convict the world of injustice (John 16). Therefore, human engagement in justice is rooted in prayerful dependency and discernment, and those who seek justice can celebrate expressions of justice wherever they are found, regardless of the human agent.

7. **God's ultimate provision of justice:** The biblical faith is rooted in confidence that one day the world will be recreated as the domain of justice. Evil, oppression, injustice, and suffering will be eliminated from the new creation. Although current expressions of justice are only partial, we persist in bold confidence knowing that all acts of justice are signs of God's coming kingdom. To enable small expressions of social justice now is to give witness to the ultimate just society yet to come. To persist in injustice is to live on the wrong side of the future.

Difference Between Social Service and Social Justice

Social Service	Social Justice
Service is done by those with power to help those without.	Justice recognizes that everyone needs for life to be made right.
Service risks diminishing recipients' dignity when resources, power and skills are "owned" by the "giver."	Justice restores human dignity by creating an environment in which all who are involved "give" and "receive."
Service is something we do for others.	Justice is something we do with others.
Service is a set of activities or an event.	Justice is a social structure and a lifestyle.
Service expects results immediately.	Justice recognizes that systemic changes take time.
The goal of service is to help others.	The goal of justice is to remove obstacles so people can help themselves.
Service focuses on what we can accomplish.	Justice focuses on how we can work with others so that life is made right.
Service focuses on symptoms of injustice	Justice addresses causes of suffering, as well as symptoms.

Adapted from *Deep Justice in a Broken World,* by Chap Clark and Kara Powell (Zondervan, 2008).